Original title:
Waves on the Horizon

Copyright © 2025 Creative Arts Management OÜ
All rights reserved.

Author: Arabella Whitmore
ISBN HARDBACK: 978-1-80581-622-5
ISBN PAPERBACK: 978-1-80581-149-7
ISBN EBOOK: 978-1-80581-622-5

A Canvas of Ocean's Lure

The ocean's playful splashes, oh what a sight,
Seagulls arguing 'bout snacks, a comical plight.
The crabs do the cha-cha, in their own little way,
While the fish gossip secrets, all through the day.

Here comes a beach ball, it rolls with a jig,
It tickles the toes of a very fat pig.
Sunscreen's a battle, where's my hat gone,
As I look like a lobster, waves won't take long!

Rhythm of the Sea

The ocean hums a silly tune,
Bubbles dance beneath the moon.
Fish in hats swim by with flair,
Seagulls squawk without a care.

Crabs play cards upon the sand,
With sandwiches all nicely planned.
Starfish laugh in hide-and-seek,
While otters giggle, feeling sleek.

Sunlit Ripples

Under the sun, the beach ball flies,
With jellyfish sporting ties.
Pelicans dive with comic grace,
Splashing waves all over the place.

A dolphin slips with loud 'Ka-boom!',
As clams decide to all make room.
Sandcastles stand with hats so tall,
Until the tide decides to brawl.

Secrets Beneath the Foam

Beneath the bubbles, secrets hide,
A clam with pearls, stitched up with pride.
Snails pothole past with epic speed,
While octopuses gossip and plead.

Mermaids swap tales, wigs on their heads,
Charting the way where the seahorse treads.
But flip-flops float in a ghostly chase,
While barnacles dance with cheeky grace.

Journey to the Edge

On a boat built from old shoelaces,
We set sail to the fishy places.
A parrot squawks, "Where's the snack?"
As our map leads to a giant whack!

With flamingos strutting and goats that cheer,
We conquer the surf with no hint of fear.
But alas! The wind changed our plan,
Now we float off to pancake land!

Where the Water Meets the Sky

The seagulls squawk, they have a plan,
To steal your fries from that poor man.
And while the fish just swim on by,
  They wonder why folks like to cry.

Reflections on the Blue

A crab wore shades, looking just so cool,
He said, "Don't bother, I'm no one's fool!"
While jellyfish glide with grace and flair,
They flip on 'gram, no self-aware.

Dancing with the Tide

With buckets out, we dig for gold,
But kids just laugh, they're wise and bold.
The sandcastles lean, a royal plight,
As waves rush in, they take a bite.

Embrace of the Elements

The sun brings warmth, and winds a breeze,
But watch your hat; it loves to tease!
A napkin flies, a feast in plight,
Yet laughter echoes deep into night.

Distant Shores Calling

Fish in tuxedos, dancing about,
Seagulls gossip, what's that all about?
A crab in sunglasses, sassy and bold,
Whispers of treasure, stories retold.

Pineapple drinks with umbrellas so bright,
Pirates in flip-flops, what a funny sight!
Under the sun, they slap on the cream,
Who knew ocean life could be such a dream?

Liquid Dreams

Mermaids with coffee, stirring up fun,
Doing cha-cha as they soak in the sun.
Octopuses juggling, hats on their heads,
Bubbles and laughter as joy fills the spreads.

Floating on noodles, it's quite quite the thrill,
Dolphins in tuxes, practicing their skill.
A beach ball escapes, chased by seals' cheer,
Life in the water, so wacky and clear.

Undercurrents of Hope

Starfish on surfboards, riding the tide,
Clouds doing backflips, oh what a ride!
A lobster in sneakers, racing the tide,
With laughs from the sea, it's a colorful ride.

Turtles in shades, selling popcorn with flair,
Jellyfish float, like they haven't a care.
Each splash of the sea brings a giggle and cheer,
In this watery world, there's nothing to fear.

Celestial Swells

Astronaut fish swimming, they'll soon hit the stars,
Counting the rockets, and dodging the cars.
Gulls on the moon, trying to find a fish,
Making a wish, oh what a silly dish!

Starry-eyed dolphins, catching the breeze,
Launching their dreams with loops and with ease.
Shimmering laughter lights up the deep,
In cosmic adventures, our grins never sleep.

Serenade of the Surf

Upon the shore, there's a dance,
Crabs in swim trunks take a chance.
Seagulls laugh in silly glee,
Diving for snacks and sipping tea.

Each wave a note in playful song,
Salty melodies that can't be wrong.
With seashells clapping in delight,
Even the fish are feeling bright.

Floating flip-flops in a race,
Chasing stories, making space.
A beach ball skips with lightened flair,
While bikini tops go for a tear.

The sun plays peek-a-boo from high,
As sunscreen slips and kids all cry.
A serenade of fun takes flight,
Where silly antics rule the night.

Swaying on the Surface

In rubber boats, we push and glide,
Our paddles cheer, they cannot hide.
Fish give a wink and swim on past,
We laugh so hard, a hearty blast.

Tangles of seaweed in our hair,
Like fashion trends we'll never wear.
With each splash, we squeal and shout,
Who knew the sea would bring about?

A dolphin slips in a neat ballet,
"Watch me spin, it's ocean play!"
We try to mimic, arms aglow,
And end up drenching folks in row.

As sunbeams wink and water sparkles,
Our silly smiles become the parcles.
Swaying gently as we float along,
The surface hums our jovial song.

The Call of the Abyss

Deep below where shadows play,
Creatures giggle in a fray.
Octopus doing the cha-cha slide,
Even plankton dance with pride.

A whale mimics our best sounds,
As submarines do silly rounds.
Starfish practice their best pose,
While jellyfish do toe-to-toe.

With bubbles rising, laughter flares,
As crabs wear hats and silly stares.
"Why so serious?" the fish all tease,
While sea turtles sway with ease.

The call of depths, a comical tune,
Where underground dance parties bloom.
Nothing serious beneath the brine,
Just playful critters feeling fine.

Hues of the Horizon

Colors splash where sea meets sky,
A canvas painted, oh my, oh my!
Crayons lost in ocean's box,
Pink dolphins dancing in their flocks.

The sunset giggles, blushes bright,
As sea otters join in the light.
With each stroke of orange and blue,
The horizon winks—it's all for you!

A toaster pops from sandy bays,
Toasting bread in salt-rimmed rays.
The seagulls flock for breakfast bites,
Dreaming of tasty seaside fights.

In hues of laughter, joy abounds,
Where skies erupt in giggling sounds.
Each color's laughter, wild and free,
A playful world where whimsy's key.

Chasing Sunbeams on the Sea

The dolphins dance in frothy delight,
Chasing their shadows, oh what a sight!
Seagulls squawk jokes, while crabs do their jig,
A beach ball rolls, and the dog barks a gig.

Sun hats are flying, oh where did they go?
Flip-flops are flopping, like fish that won't flow.
Kids in the sand are building a castle,
But watch out for the tide, it's quite a hassle!

Ice creams are melting, what a sticky scene,
Chocolate chip sundaes, oh how they gleam!
The sun winks down as the sunscreen's applied,
"Did you miss a spot?" is the funniest slide.

So we laugh and we splash till the day's nearly done,
With sand in our shorts, we still call it fun!
As the sun dips low, we all wave goodbye,
To tomfoolery's end, as the gulls in the sky.

Fading Moments in Coastal Glow

The tide pulls back, waves in retreat,
With sand between toes that can't stand the heat.
Jellyfish drift like balloons on the run,
While toddlers chase them, thinking it's fun.

The beach towels billow, a colorful sea,
As sunscreen fights battles on backs, oh so free!
A crab scuttles by in a hurry to flee,
"Excuse me!" it shouts, "Outta the way, let me be!"

The sunset brings laughter, what a curious sight,
With marshmallows roasting, oh what pure delight!
"Last s'more!" we shout, a race for the treat,
But the fire's more slippery than a fish in the heat.

So here's to the moments that make us all grin,
In fading dusk light, let the fun times begin!
With stories retold and laughter that swells,
As stars start to twinkle, and night casts its spells.

The Rhythm of Liquid Dreams

Bubbles dance in the air,
Seagulls steal a sandwich flair.
Sandcastles made of wet socks,
Don't you dare knock off my rocks.

Surfboards tumble like old hats,
Fish hold high-wire acrobat chats.
Tides come in like a big, fuzzy dog,
Chasing after a slippery frog.

Chubby crabs in tiny suits,
Doing the cha-cha in slick boots.
Jellyfish wearing fancy ties,
Throwing parties where no one dies.

A lighthouse hums a silly tune,
Braving storms, strutting like a loon.
Liquid dreams swirl out of reach,
While sand men gather for a speech.

Lighthouses and Untamed Horizons

There's a beacon shining bright,
Guiding ships towards a snack bite.
Seagulls argue over a fry,
While dolphins practice their sly cry.

Octopus wears a funny hat,
Telling fish tales, imagine that!
The tide tickles the little boats,
As barnacles watch from their coats.

Sandwiches fly through the air,
As clams sit grumpy in despair.
A crab with shades strolls by with flair,
Laughing loud and not a care.

With each sunset, we all cheer,
For surf and sun that brings good cheer.
Life's a jest on this folly swing,
In the laughter, the sea takes wing.

Splashes of a Forgotten Dawn

Before breakfast, the ocean stirs,
Whispers of laughter from the surf blur.
Toast done, oh the jelly spills,
Mermans' treasure of ancient thrills.

Children dance with drip and slip,
Sandy toes in wild flip-flip.
Seashells giggle, riding high,
While sand and sunscreen wave goodbye.

Starfish on a picnic quest,
Crabs argue who's the very best.
A rubber duck floats past my ear,
Chasing dreams we once held dear.

As the sun begins to play,
Fish doing ballet in the spray.
Each splash a story yet untold,
In the laughter, our hearts unfold.

The Call of the Endless Blue

In a pool, a whirling race,
Rubber ducks find their sweet place.
The tides tease with bubbly glee,
Floating dreams beneath the sea.

A whale dons shades, cracking jokes,
Sea cucumbers playing the folks.
With flip-flops worn all awry,
The sun swoops down, oh my, oh my!

Oysters with their fancy cleats,
Dancing to rhythmic drumming beats.
The horizon winks, with a big grin,
While mermaids twirl in spins of sin.

As the day melts like ice cream,
We all gather for one last dream.
The echo of laughter as we dive,
In this silly dance, we feel alive!

Harmony in the Liquid Realm

Fish waltz beneath the sun,
Dancing like they've just won.
Seaweed sways in a silly way,
Laughing as crabs try to play.

Jellyfish float with a glow,
Singing songs they don't even know.
The octopus plays hide and seek,
With eight arms that are quite unique.

A dolphin tells a corny joke,
All the fish just laugh and choke.
The seabed's a stage for all to see,
Reef parties are the best, whee!

So raise your fins, join the fun,
In the liquid realm, everyone's done.
With giggles bubbling all around,
The silliest joys in the deep are found.

Journey to the Edge of Blue

Setting sail on a bright, clear day,
Seagulls squawk, making merry play.
The ship's cat thinks she's the queen,
As she struts about, oh so serene.

A sailor slips, and the crew all cheer,
Splashing water, oh dear, oh dear!
Bubbles rise like giggling clowns,
As they float up, wearing frowns.

The compass spins in a funny dance,
Leading us in a kooky prance.
Mermaids laugh with laughter bright,
Waving tails in pure delight.

Under the sun and the big blue sky,
Adventure calls, we're flying high!
With a merry heart, let's blur the line,
To the edge of blue, it's cocktail time.

Flickering Lights on Distant Waves

Stars are twinkling in the dark,
Little fish try to make a mark.
One says, 'Look, I'm a shooting star!'
The others laugh, 'You're not that far!'

The lighthouse blinks a cheesy grin,
While crabs build towers from within.
A glowstick fish leads the parade,
Making sure fun will never fade.

A turtle tries to moonwalk too,
Stumbling like he's had a brew.
The ocean giggles, waves in tow,
A comedy show down below.

So when the night is fun and bright,
Join the laughter, dance with delight!
In flickering lights, the joy won't cease,
Every splash, a bit of peace.

Interlude of the Deep Silence

The ocean sleeps in a gentle hush,
But the clams are making quite a fuss.
'Clap your shells!' one clam does shout,
While the others ponder what it's about.

A starfish grins, it's all a joke,
While sea cucumbers quietly poke.
They joke of treasure, lost and found,
While sardines swirl all around.

Turtles yawn, not one bit shy,
While seahorses play, oh my, oh my!
With a giggle here and a smile there,
The ocean's joy is everywhere.

So in this deep beneath the foam,
Silly moments will always roam.
In silence thick, laughter gleams,
Underwater dreams, where joy redeems.

Lullabies of the Lagoon

In the lagoon, fish dance with glee,
A frog croaks a tune, off-key as can be.
The lily pads bob like boats in a race,
While turtles take naps, dreaming of space.

Crabs do the cha-cha, unaware of the tide,
And snails are the judges, they giggle and slide.
There's laughter aplenty, the sun's shining bright,
As seagulls squawk jokes that take flight in delight.

Starlit Waters

Under the sparkle, the fish wear a hat,
They gather for stories, and one is a cat!
"Now listen," says Sassy, "the moon's gone astray,
He tripped on a starlight and danced on the bay."

The night is a scene, with laughter and fun,
As otters are racing, 'til day has begun.
The tide tickles toes, while the breeze plays a tune,
As friends all unite, 'neath the glow of the moon.

Mists of Morning

In the morning mist, a surprise awaits,
A fish in pajamas arrives at the gates.
With breakfast of shrimp, they gather in droves,
To gossip and giggle in their cozy little groves.

The turtles complain, "This fog is absurd!
I can't find my breakfast, it's all quite a blur!"
A pelican swoops, with a laugh and a flap,
And steals all their snacks for a mid-morning nap.

The Infinite Expanse

In the deep blue, a fishy parade,
With sharks in sunglasses, a finned masquerade.
They swim past a whale, who's working on mime,
Creating a scene to stand the test of time.

A crab in a top hat takes center stage,
Declaring the sea, an ocean of age.
Yet laughter erupts, as they all join the dance,
Forget about worries, it's a funny romance.

A Melody in Coastal Breezes

The seagulls dance like they're in a band,
Singing tunes in the soft golden sand.
You'd swear they're crooning a catchy refrain,
While a crab moonwalks, to a tune in his brain.

The sun has a laugh, it's wearing a grin,
As the flip-flops leap, getting tossed in the din.
Each splash from the shore, a giggle set free,
Nature's own jester, a sight to see!

A clam shells out jokes, with a chuckle and jest,
While kids build their castles, in a tropical fest.
The breeze plays the harp, with salty delight,
As the tide waves hello, in cheerful respite.

In this seaside circus, all silly and bold,
The ocean's pure humor, never gets old.
Laughter floats lightly on the bright sunny bay,
A melody thriving in frolicsome play.

The Song of the Salty Spirit

A fish in a tux, so dapper and sly,
Practices ballet while the dolphins all fly.
The octopus juggles with ease, what a show!
While the seaweed sways, saying, 'Go, go, go!'

A whale hums a tune that echoes the deep,
As starfish snap selfies, while gulls take a leap.
With every good splash, the world shares a grin,
Even the crabs do a cha-cha spin!

The coral's all gossiping, colors so bright,
With sea cucumbers sharing their fright.
Anemones giggle at fish passing by,
In a sea of humor, they float and they sigh.

Above, the sun chuckles, with rays full of cheer,
Casting jokes on the waves, it's the time of the year.
In this salty domain, we dance day and night,
With a spirit that sparkles, pure joy in the light.

Tranquility in the Midst of Swells

A turtle in flip-flops, so chill and so grand,
He sunbathes with purpose, a master of sand.
While the sea turtle memes go viral, you see,
In a beachside lounge chair, sipping iced tea.

Beneath, where the squids hold their nightly review,
They debate about flavors, of black or of blue.
A crab with a monocle, orchestrates peace,
While fish create bubbles that never will cease.

The gentle waves giggle, rolling in light,
Tickling the coast with a mischievous bite.
Seashells share rumors from far-off domain,
As the sand dollars laugh at their moneyless gain.

And as sleepy sun sets with whimsical flair,
The dolphins form lines, for a limbo affair.
Tranquility dances on this sandy stage,
With laughter and silliness filling each page.

A Breath Between the Ebb and Flow

The ocean winks playfully with blisters in foam,
It's a jester's delight, calling all to roam.
Barnacles cheer, 'We're the best at our game!'
While the eel sneaks a peek, then giggles in shame.

The tide rolls back out, like a child at a feast,
With the flotsam and jetsam now dancing, at least.
A clam yells, "Free hugs!" to those passing by,
As the pelicans squawk, in their comical cry.

Every grain of sand holds a story so grand,
Of fish who hold banquets, and seashells unplanned.
The dolphins put on a slapstick display,
With flips and with flops, they brighten the day.

As night falls, the stars burst with light laughter,
Sparkling mischief, for the moon's glowing master.
In this ebb and flow, joy never will murk,
Each breath is a giggle, the sea's endless perk.

Secrets Beneath the Surface

Bubbles pop like little jokes,
Fish are laughing, making pokes.
Seaweed sways in rhythmic dance,
Who knew an octopus had romance?

Crabs throw parties, do the cha-cha,
While starfish argue, 'No, you're the star!'
Anemones tickle with gentle embrace,
Underwater humor fills the space.

Turtles wearing shades, looking cool,
Surfing shells, like they rule the pool.
Seahorses giggle, tails entwined,
Ocean's comedy is one of a kind!

Meditation of the Moonlit Waters

Under the moon, the water gleams,
Fish tell secrets, share their dreams.
A seal barks in a funny tone,
While bubbles rise like thoughts alone.

Mermaids play charades in the mist,
Oh, that fish, he can't resist!
Tangles of kelp, a messy affair,
But they shrug it off, like they don't care.

A clockfish ticking, losing track,
Time flies by, they never look back.
In this night, so bright and clear,
Every splash reveals a cheer.

The Secret Life of the Current

Currents giggle, swirling fast,
They learn the past, forget at last.
Rolling rocks with playful grace,
As they dart, they leave a trace.

Eels doing the worm, quite the sight,
Nudging fish, 'You think you're right?'
An octopus dons a funny hat,
While turtles joke, 'Hey, check that spat!'

Whirlpools winking, having fun,
Chasing sunbeams, one by one.
Together they're a jolly crew,
If oceans talk, they'd laugh with you!

Echoes of a Serene Vastness

The sea whispers jokes at dawn,
Echoes dance, then swiftly gone.
Tides tell tales of ships once brave,
But fish just roll their eyes and wave.

Seagulls giggle at fishermen's plight,
Casting nets with all their might.
But the fish swim round, making quips,
Dodge and weave, giving flips.

Rays of sunlight paint the scene,
While crabs strut in a funny routine.
Life's a jest beneath the sun,
In endless laughter, we all run.

Portals to the Celestial Sands

Underneath the sun's bright glance,
The beachgoers begin their dance.
With buckets, shovels, laughter loud,
They build a kingdom, proud and cowed.

Seagulls swoop, they steal a fry,
While kids all scream and almost cry.
Sandcastles stand with globby flair,
Their towers wobble in salty air.

Tide Pools of Twilight Stories

In pools of wonder, shells abide,
A crab with sass begins to glide.
It waves its claws like it's a king,
While starfish judge, "What's that thing?"

With each small splash, a fishy muse,
Bubbles rise, with giggles infused.
The tales unfold in salty notes,
As squids take turns in silly boats.

The Glistening Sighs of Dawn

As dawn arrives with sleepy yawns,
The ocean hums its glittering songs.
Surfers tumble, then they gleam,
Face-planting in a salty dream.

A seagull laughs at clumsy feats,
While dolphins mock with playful beats.
The morning light glints and flicks,
As sandmen giggle, making tricks.

Traces of the Celestial Waters

Footprints dance along the shore,
Chasing crabs who run for cover.
A splash! A shout! Oh, what a scene,
As kids make ripples, bright and keen.

The tide pulls back, a comical race,
Chasing seaweed; such a disgrace!
In laughter's grip, they turn and lean,
As chaos reigns on this sandy screen.

Beyond the Crest

The seagulls squawk, a lively crew,
On boats that bob like balloons anew.
Fish tales grow tall, as they always do,
'Caught a whopper!'—just the usual view.

Splashing about, the sun starts to tease,
While flip-flops fly with a touch of ease.
Someone screams, 'Look out!' but who can please,
The fish that giggle and swim under trees.

Shadows over the Bay

The crabs in the sand are having a ball,
Dancing like they're at some wild hall.
One wears a hat, way too big and tall,
While others just shuffle, and trip, and fall.

Life slows down as the tides take a trip,
With lemonade splashes, it's quite a script.
The sun sipping joy, takes a happy slip,
While kids build castles—their dreams start to flip.

Sailing Through the Mist

There's a parrot with jokes, perched high in the rig,
'Why'd the fish blush?' 'I don't know, dig!'
With sails full of laughter, they spin and jig,
While dolphins giggle, 'We're feeling quite big!'

The compass spins wild, like a dancer's stance,
'Hold tight!' they say, 'It's a nautical dance!'
The fog rolls in thick, but watch how they prance,
'The sea's just a stage, come join the romance!'

The Dance of the Dawn

Morning breaks loose with a coffee delight,
The sun yawns wide, stretching into sight.
Birds in a chorus, sing with pure fright,
As fishermen giggle, 'We'll get it right!'

On surfboards they wobble, it's quite the sight,
Every splash gets a cheer, what pure delight!
'Don't feed the sharks!' is the common fright,
But they just want laughs, not a bite in sight!

Ripples Across the Distant Blue

In the ocean's grand ballet, they skip,
Fish wear a bubble-wrap for a trip.
Seagulls steal snacks, no chance to confide,
While crabs play it cool, with nowhere to hide.

Jellyfish float like they run the show,
Doing the limbo, moving real slow.
Sandy flip-flops launch on a spree,
Whispering jokes with sand-covered glee.

Hot sun above, and kids run to play,
Splashing each other in a silly display.
Seashells gather secrets, giggles combined,
While dolphins huddle, with humor combined.

Laughter rings out, as tides start to tease,
Little fish dance, aiming to please.
Sunsets follow suit, with colors that blend,
And all of the sea creatures just pretend.

A Journey to the Edge of Aqua

A curious turtle in a top hat sashays,
Waving hello in his quirky ways.
Mermaids sing tunes off-key from the reef,
As ships pretend their hulls aren't in grief.

A crab with a monocle sips from a cup,
Complaining the currents are all mixed up.
While starfish discuss their latest round,
Of gossip that's heard all over the ground.

In the distance, a whale makes a splash,
Carrying jokes that cause quite a crash.
Fish gather 'round with wide-open eyes,
For tales of the sea and its fishy lies.

And as the day fades, they laugh and they cheer,
While waves hold their breath, they're in on the cheer.
With laughter carried on a salty breeze,
Their joy echoes under the dancing seas.

Dreams in the Tidal Flow

Oysters dreaming of pearls in a nightlight,
While clams shy away, fearing the spotlight.
The surf hums tunes, a ticklish refrain,
As dolphins play games, a splashy campaign.

Sea urchins chat of their spiky charms,
Sharing hot gossip of their ocean farms.
Starfish take selfies, they're quite full of pride,
Though their poses get tricky when they try a glide.

A pelican drops in for snacks in the sun,
Big fish swim by, saying, "That's not fun!"
But laughter erupts with a flick of a tail,
As ripples of joy set the mood without fail.

Night unfolds its blanket, stars twinkle bright,
As creatures tell stories with sheer delight.
And in this aquatic circus galore,
The dreams wash ashore, begging for more.

Beneath the Coral Sky

Beneath a painted sky, corals break dance,
Epic routines while fish take a chance.
Clownfish in make-up, bright as a ray,
Consider themselves stars on this crazy display.

Seahorses strut in their slick little suits,
Belly dancing crabs show off their new roots.
With laughter that bubbles through turquoise scenes,
They twirl in the currents, like animated machines.

Anemones giggle, tickling the sand,
While turtles wear shades, looking oh-so grand.
A parade of excitement drifts through the sea,
Bringing joy through ripples, wild and free.

As the night falls down, stars take their place,
Creating a shimmering, soft, playful grace.
In the ocean's embrace, the humor won't fade,
For fun's just a splash away, masquerade!

Echoes Beyond the Shoreline

Seagulls laugh in the bright blue,
Chasing crabs like they've lost their shoe.
Shells dance in the sand, a wild parade,
While fish plot mischief in their ice cream shade.

A flip-flop flung, ten feet in the air,
Splashing a surfer's unwelcome affair.
The tides giggle softly, a silly tease,
As the sun winks and the dolphins sneeze.

Kites soar high, as kids try to run,
Sandcastles crumbling, oh, ain't this fun!
With buckets and shovels, we make a mess,
Then we're buried, laughter's all we possess.

At twilight, the jokes from the beach commence,
With tales of sand monsters and no common sense.
As moonbeams twinkle on this silly night,
The echoes keep laughing, oh what a sight!

The Serenade of Salty Breezes

A breeze tickles noses, oh what a prank,
Blowing hats off that bright beach drank.
The seafoam giggles, bubbles on the run,
Yelling 'catch me!' while the sun has fun.

Sunbathers lounging, trying to tan,
While a curious crab steals a sandwich plan.
Flip-flops flopping, a sudden surprise,
One gets away, under everyone's cries.

Laughter and splashes, the joy never ends,
As sand sticks to legs of unwary friends.
A jellyfish floats in a fabulous dance,
While kids try to leap, strike the funniest stance.

As night falls down, the stars start to play,
Glimmers of laughter light up the bay.
The salty breeze whispers, 'Stay here, my friend,'
In a lullaby giggle that never will end.

Murmurs Beneath the Dusk

Under the sunset, shadows take flight,
As beach towels become a noodle fight.
Mom yells, 'Stop!' while dad can't control,
The splash of the water and the dog's silly roll.

Sandpeople rising, a castle of dreams,
With moats full of giggles, bursting at the seams.
Sticks transformed into swords, all the rage,
While crabs playking dom, they're quick on the stage.

S'mores by the fire, with chocolate glints,
Marshmallows turn pirates with sticky hints.
Stories of fish that escaped every hook,
Made up by grandpa, the best little book.

The moon joins the fun, a bright, silly chap,
Cracking up softly as we share our nap.
Murmurs in the dusk, secrets the sea keeps,
With laughter of memories, it cushions our sleeps.

Reflections in the Aqua Veil

Pool toys float lazy, a flamingo ballet,
While water splashes, oh hip hip hooray!
Rubber duck tactics, an orange attack,
Who'll save the treasures from the kids' fun rack?

Noodles become swords, battles we wage,
Fighting for glory, our own splash page.
Giggles erupt as someone gets tossed,
In the aqua veil, no worries get lost.

The sun dips low, painting skies with zest,
While shadows dance, it's a playful fest.
Coconut drinks cheer us, the laughing delight,
Beneath the stars twinkling, a magical night.

Under this canvas, we gather and weave,
With memories so bright, it's hard to believe.
Reflections of joy ripple sweet through the air,
In the aqua veil's laughter, we'll always share.

Calling of the Unseen Depths

A fish in a tux, I saw last night,
Dancing under the pale moonlight.
With moves so slick, he stole the show,
Said he'd swim fast, but his tummy said 'no!'

The crabs threw a party, they lost their grip,
In tiny red hats, they began to slip.
They twirled and swirled, gave the starfish a fright,
As they cha-cha cha'd till the morning light.

An octopus joined, with eight legs to spare,
He played the guitar, with quite a flair.
But when he strummed, he dropped the pick,
And wriggled around like a rubbery trick!

So here's to the depths, so silly and bright,
Where fish throw raves, in the soft, moonlit night.
Their laughter bubbles, so carefree and bold,
In a world of frolic, their tales unfold.

The Breath of the Eternal Sea

I met a seagull, named Larry the Great,
Who said he'd become, a real dinner plate!
With unending jokes, he squawked and flapped,
Claiming the fish just didn't get zapped!

On a floaty log, a turtle named Frank,
Said he'd set sail, end up on a plank.
But after two hours, he fell asleep,
Dreaming of seaweed and secrets to keep.

The dolphins jumped high, with flips and spouts,
Claimed they'd outsmart, all the silly doubts.
But each grand leap, met with a splash,
And they all landed, in a jellyfish clash!

Down by the shore, where laughter sings,
Creatures abound, wearing silly bling.
In a bubble party, as bright as it seems,
They dance with the waves, in their silliest dreams.

Fables of the Cresting Foam

In a tale full of bubbles, a crab played the role,
He fancied himself as a rock and roll soul.
Clapping his claw, he struck quite a pose,
While his friend, the shrimp, just hid his nose.

A sea urchin once told, a joke with great glee,
About clams who were shy, and wouldn't agree.
They'd clack and they'd chatter, but never a peep,
Just digging their shells, in a secretive heap!

When otters glide by, in their talents so slick,
They juggle the seaweed, with an oceanic trick.
But when one goes splat, on a slippery dock,
The laughter erupts, as the tides mock the mock!

In the foam and the fun, let the stories arise,
A medley of creatures, under the skies.
Each ripple a giggle, each splash a cheer,
As the ocean narrates, tales loud and clear.

Beyond where the Light Dances

There's a pirate with patches, who's lost his way,
He's trading his maps, for a jar of sea hay.
Claiming the fortune of an underwater chest,
But forgets it's the fish, who eat all the best!

A mermaid named Lucy, with a flute and a grin,
Plays songs to the walruses to tickle their chin.
But when they get groovy, and start to sway,
Lucy just swims off, saying 'not today!'

A squid in a bowtie throws parties galore,
Invites all the critters, then snaps the door.
When they all surface, with giggles and cheer,
He yells, 'Not so fast, the punch isn't here!'

Yet laughter erupts, beyond all the gloss,
In a sea full of jests, where chaos is boss.
So when light dances bright, on the water's sway,
Laughing is timeless, in a comical play.

Beneath the Churning Veil

Underneath that frothy sheet,
The fishes dance with silly feet.
They wear their hats and sing a tune,
A jellyfish joins, under the moon.

Crabs debate the best crab cake,
While seagulls plot a sneaky take.
The starfish try to star in plays,
But end up napping all their days.

Dolphins laugh, they leap and spin,
Playing tag with their fin-ny kin.
A clam throws pearls, it's quite a show,
Who knew sea life had such flow?

Beneath the tides, the jokes flow free,
As everyone giggles in salty glee.
The ocean's punchlines, always a hit,
In this watery world, laughter's a wit!

Song of the Ocean's Heart

Bubbles burst with giggles sweet,
As crabs parade on tiny feet.
The ocean hums a catchy tune,
With fishy dreams that make us swoon.

Octopus plays a game of chess,
With seaweed making quite a mess.
A starfish shouts, 'I'm the best!'
And all the sea critters are impressed.

The whales come in with booming laughs,
Telling tales of ancient staffs.
While plankton practice their ballet,
And mermaids cheer 'Hip-hip-hooray!'

Each splash a note, a quirky song,
The ocean's heart sings all night long.
With playful beats that make us sway,
In this sea of laughter, we'll stay and play!

The Canvas Beyond the Breakers

Pictures painted by splashing foam,
A canvas made where fish call home.
Crabs with paints, and brush in claws,
Creating art that earns applause.

Gulls are curators of this show,
Chattering loudly, 'Look at that glow!'
A mermaid's hair, a colorful blend,
It's hard to tell where art will end.

Seahorses strut like fashion stars,
Posing proudly beneath the Mars.
Jellybeans float like artful fluff,
In this sea where life's just tough.

The canvas swirls with hues so bright,
Each splash and swirl a pure delight.
In salty laughter, they do create,
A masterpiece that'll captivate!

Starlit Paths on Liquid Glass

Under starlight, fish take a stroll,
Guided by moonbeams, that's their goal.
They trip on jelly, slip, and slide,
In this cosmic parade, they take pride.

A turtle wearing a tiny cap,
Critiques the stars with a hearty laugh.
While otters play their silly games,
Diving deep, calling each other's names.

Shimmering paths in the playful night,
Where laughter echoes with pure delight.
Anemones wiggle to a funky beat,
While dolphins spin and dive, so neat!

With every splash, a joke unspools,
As fishy friends break all the rules.
In this world, where giggles rise,
Under starlit skies, merriment flies!

Chasing the Ocean's Breath

In a boat made of dreams and a snack,
We set sail with sandwiches stacked,
The seagulls laughed, what a silly crew,
As we splashed about, tasting ocean stew.

With fishing rods twisted like our fate,
We chased fish that were far too late,
They winked at us from a safe retreat,
While we just bobbed, a comical feat.

A crab with a top hat joined the ride,
He danced on deck, full of pride,
We offered him chips, he couldn't refuse,
Life is a joke, oh what fun we choose!

Sunset arrives, painting skies brown,
We toasted our luck in this merry town,
With dreams of big fish and tales that tease,
Tomorrow's voyage, a laugh to seize.

Secrets in the Salted Breeze

The breeze whispers secrets of fishy delight,
To a nose that twitches at the salty bite,
I bent to listen, but tripped on a shell,
Fell face-first, now I'm part of the swell!

Dancing with crabs like they're my fan club,
They tag along, what a hilarious hub,
I spin, I twirl, what a comical scene,
To the rhythm of waves, they know I'm the queen!

A fish with a top hat swam by with a frown,
'See my bowtie?' he said, flipping around,
I chuckled aloud, 'You're dapper, it's true,
But my swimsuit's got stripes, who's best, me or you?'

As night draped a blanket of stars overhead,
We shared our worries with jellyfish bread,
In this salty realm where the laughter won't fade,
What tales we'd tell on the ocean parade!

Where the Sky Meets the Sea

The sky dropped a pancake right into my boat,
With syrup of sunshine, oh what a gloat,
I grabbed my fork, ready for a feast,
But the seagulls swooped, and my joy decreased!

A dolphin appeared, his grin bright and wide,
'Join my party!' he beckoned with pride,
We danced in circles, the fish were aghast,
As I tried catching them, but they swam past!

Clouds threw a party, a fluffy parade,
While I tried to juggle with some seaweed made,
The ocean roared laughter, what a funny sight,
As I dropped each piece, and they took flight!

Even the sun chuckled, a golden tease,
Watching my antics from high with great ease,
In this comical dance where the fun never ends,
Weird friends and laughter, oh how it blends!

The Lullaby of the Blue Expanse

Napping on sands with a starfish for a hat,
Dreaming of pizza and that chubby cat,
The tide came in, played a funny tune,
While I snoozed snugly, under the moon!

The ocean hummed softly, a lullaby strange,
Of fish in tuxedos, preparing for change,
They waltzed in the depths, all swanky and neat,
While my dreams bubbled up, a bubbling treat!

A hermit crab shouted, 'I'm hosting a ball!'
I rolled my eyes, 'Does it have snacks at all?'
He shrugged and began to salsa with flair,
While I popped up to join without a care!

As night wrapped us gently in shimmering light,
We danced with the stars, oh what a delight,
In this silly tale of the vast azure sea,
We sang our own lullabies, as happy as can be!

Remnants of the Daylight Dance

The sun tripped over its own feet,
As shadows jived, oh what a feat!
Grasshoppers wore their finest shoes,
And dared the daisies to cut loose.

Laughter bubbled from the brook,
As croaking frogs gave the world a look.
They strutted and hopped with gleeful pride,
While butterflies cheered from the side.

Clouds rolled in like playful beasts,
Joining the jig, they raved at least.
The sky became a big dance floor,
While the wind twirled and craved more.

As daylight wore its silly hat,
Dust bunnies giggled, imagine that!
With every twirl, they made offbeat sounds,
A party where joy forever abounds.

Fluctuations of the Ocean's Essence

The sea tried to wear a fancy dress,
But tangled seaweed said 'No mess!'
Crabs scuttled sideways, flipped with glee,
While fish held auditions for an odd musical spree.

Seagulls squawked a tuneless song,
While starfish twirled a dance so wrong.
Jellyfish bobbed like they were high,
Swaying gently under the blue sky.

Sandcastles popped up like wild mushrooms,
As waves crashed down, making them tombs.
But do not fret, they rise again,
And thus the cycle does pretend.

The ocean giggles in frothy white,
As surfboards chase the dreams of flight.
With every splash and foamy cheer,
The water whispers, 'No worries here!'

Reflections in a Shimmering Pool

Stillness ripples within the glass,
Frogs suit up for a game of sass.
Tadpoles practice their swimming race,
While dragonflies strut in their fine lace.

The sun wears shades, looking all cool,
As fish swap gossip, breaking the rule.
They share tales of the giant net,
And the one that got away, no regret.

A duck paddles by with elegant grace,
Checking for splashes, just in case.
But a splash from below steals the show,
The pool's laughing so loud, don't you know?

Even the reeds lean in to hear,
What secrets the water holds dear.
With every ripple, a giggle is found,
In the shimmering pool that knows no bounds.

Passages Through Time's Embrace

Tick tock, said the clock on the wall,
As time stumbled, it began to sprawl.
A cat took a nap on yesterday's news,
While memories danced in their favorite shoes.

Yesterday joined hands with today,
Playing hopscotch, oh what a display!
Tomorrow peeked with a cheeky grin,
Saying, 'Hold my drink, let the fun begin!'

Echoes of laughter stretched like a kite,
While shadows played hide and seek at night.
Moments slipped by like butter on toast,
A sweet, silly dance we cherish the most.

As hours waltz in the bright daylight,
Clocks turn events into pure delight.
With every tick, a chuckle ignites,
In this quirky voyage of timeless flights.

www.ingramcontent.com/pod-product-compliance
Lightning Source LLC
Chambersburg PA
CBHW072135070526
44585CB00016B/1696